ON ETHICS

❖

THOMAS L. MUINZER

❖

Belfast
LAPWING

First Published by Lapwing Publications
c/o 1, Ballysillan Drive
Belfast BT14 8HQ
lapwing.poetry@ntlworld.com
www.lapwingpoetry.com

Since before 1632
The Greig sept of the MacGregor Clan
Has been printing and binding books

Lapwing Publications are printed at Kestrel Print
Unit 1, Spectrum Centre
Shankill Road Belfast BT13 3AA
028 90 319211
E:kestrelprint@btconnect.com
Hand-bound in Belfast at the Winepress
Set in Aldine 721 BT

ISBN 978-1-907276-76-7

CONTENTS

PREFACE

This booklet was written in Belfast, in 2004, for The Knights of the Round Table Arts Collective.

When I was a second year BA student in the English Department at Queen's University Belfast, I always looked forward to running into a few particular acquaintances around campus that I had met at random - I had my regular run of friends and classmates, but these few were different; they were eccentric, free thinking, passionate, and they were all enrolled in different departments to mine. We always had great conversations each time we got chatting, and over time I came to find that, as well as taking to them as interesting people in their own right, I also had a lot in common with each of them in one way or other. Certain things I was learning at college, certain experiences I was having, were sitting difficultly with me, and if I mentioned this to pals in my class they either didn't seem to get what I meant or just weren't bothered; but these few people did get what I meant, and they were bothered. I soon got into the habit of encouraging them to come together at Chapters Café next to the Queen's School of Music. Here we would sit around whatever free table we could find amid the hubbub discussing this and that about university life, all the while coming to be increasingly good mates.

Over the course of about a year our coffee-fuelled weekly chats had culminated in the formation of a literary group, which, under the guise (at that time) of anonymity, we elaborately named The Knights of the Round Table. Out of this small seed planted at the coffee table many things have blossomed across Belfast, including the flourishing drama group Theatre Knights, the Knight Writers literary group, the Nights at the Round Table book group, the Knights Art Group, the Knights Nights (the group's bi-monthly public events that are still continuously held to this day some five years since they started), and so on.

As an Arts group, we were, naturally, concerned for the most part with the Arts and Arts matters, and we quickly found ourselves coming into line with Aestheticism, the late Victorian Arts movement that upheld pleasure and Beauty as the two great artistic ideals. Aestheticism caught perfectly the spirit of the things we were reacting against; against much of the received wisdom of academia, against the ivory towers of universities, their incumbent confining theories, and subsequent lack of contact with everyday life as a lived process. Aestheticism was all for reinstating the importance of the Arts for the sake of the pleasure and significance of the Arts themselves, not for the sake of some ugly university grade, degree or the like.

Aestheticism also insisted that Art was very important, it really mattered. It was easy, my pals and I noticed, to say why doctors are important, or politicians, or economists, but it seemed at times as if the world was in the habit of forgetting that the Arts were vitally important too, and that there were special reasons for this importance. We wanted to affirm the importance of the Arts, to fight for the Arts. And so the spirit of common discontent felt by my café pals and myself caused us to drift towards the old-fashioned position of the Victorian 'aesthete'. This was a very fun, exciting time for us. Sometimes we liked to use the word Aestheticist because it was new and it felt as if we owned it and could colour it with the meanings we wanted.

Though Aestheticism was right in many ways, it was also outmoded, and because I was the literary student in our café circle, it became my job to update it and reconfigure its wisdoms for our current times whilst putting together some sort of philosophical outcry on behalf of our coffee table gang that would embody our values and make a case for the ultimate importance of the Arts. The result was *On Ethics*.

On Ethics, written some years back now when the present writer was a young idealist, is a pleasure-filled philosophy; it enjoys 'the undeniable fact that we all, being human, have a remarkable capacity for pleasure', and celebrates the belief that 'as long as a person retains a sense of rational dignity, and keeps a sensible, considerate head on his or her shoulders, the pleasure-seeker must be allowed to embrace life's joys without guilt, without hindrance, and with a great sense of delight.' Now and again matters particular to Northern Ireland are touched on in order to give things an immediacy for Belfast, which is where my friends and I were based as Queen's students, but broadly speaking the booklet aims to stay general.

The 'Twisting of a Rope' section considers some of the pleasure/Beauty/ethics-based issues raised by Aestheticism, asserting that 'the world is Good, and human existence itself is a type of goodness. Secondly, Beauty is central to existence, and the appreciation of pleasure is a chief purpose in life. Thirdly, we have a moral obligation to try and do what will have the best possible outcome for those who are affected by our actions, which means that a pleasure-thirst should be tempered by the common-sense moral considerateness we've described as rational dignity.'

The Knights rebelled against academia's use of systems, which, we held, relentlessly dumbed down reality whilst also robbing a given individual of his or her uniqueness:

Systems are the great generalisers of Western thought; and since each Individual is complex and diverse, we are continually reminded, therefore, of the great inadequacies that are part and parcel of all systems. Systems can be very helpful, and are, indeed, vital to civilised life, but they are also in the unwavering habit of robbing us of much more truth than they reveal as they generalise infinite variety into minute, finite categories.

I was keen to hammer this home; 'the person who can generalise great sweeping laws that will explain away society does not exist, has never existed, and can never exist.' To me, and my café friends, who were all being taught the thought systems of Marxism, gender theory, and so on - just as students are at the present moment - the systems being foisted on us were all wrong, and a sort of compromise between many of them seemed to point a way towards the truth they were obscuring:

Indubitably, Marxism, gender theory, post-colonialism, gay and lesbian theory (etc.) are all independently wrong. In reality, a sort of compromise, in the context of these ideas at any rate, is probably ideal: class, gender, race, sexuality, and so forth, all have a place in our understandings of our modern condition. Certainly, no approach is entirely right, and therefore, used in a totalising way, each approach is entirely wrong.

Modern academia was (is) also relentlessly instilling the idea into its students that who we are is determined entirely by the society and culture around us. We wanted to remind people that this is only right to a point, that there are still transcendent human qualities that rise above differing social and cultural settings that are both of an intellectual and a physical kind (see 'The Individual').

The writing, of course, is coloured by the hues of Aestheticism, and after being introduced in 'The Twisting of a Rope' Aestheticism is brought back in at the 'Binary Opposition' section as a philosophical tool whilst it is being debated as a literary Art concept. In the 'Catharsis' section Aestheticism is moving towards a closing reconfiguration, and so the booklet rounds off into New Aestheticism, which summarises the New Aestheticism that the early Knights put into practice in establishing an Arts group that now, six years on, we are delighted to say has for a long time occupied its place at the very heart of the post-Troubles Belfast Arts community and has touched a good couple of hundred people who would be happy to describe themselves as part of the Knights team.

TL Muinzer
(Belfast 2010)
President, Knights of the Round Table Arts Collective

ON ETHICS

THE TWISTING OF A ROPE

In this book I intend to furnish the reader with an introduction to a type of thought I will be describing ultimately as New Aestheticism. I will be presenting an approach to Ethics, via this New Aestheticism, that will affirm the Arts as being amongst the most important, if not the most important, of human disciplines.

When dealing with a series of ideas we often hear thoughts being compared to threads or strings. We might 'string an argument together', or we might 'follow a thread of thought' or a 'line of thinking'. My preferred metaphor is a rope. Unlike a mere thread, a rope is strong, and its strength makes it extremely useful. Our rope will be put to the test in these pages for hauling at the mainsails of pre-existing philosophical thought, for tugging at the mizzenmasts that prop up our vision of morality, for battening down our hatches as we sail along troubled straights into the very eye of the hurricane of Good and Evil.

To give our metaphor a little Irish flavour, let's allow our rope to be of the flaxen sort common in olden day Ireland. The traditional Irish weaving method is a straightforward one: yarns of golden flax are wound into great thread-like strands, the strands are twisted skilfully in and out of one another, and the lines are drawn tight as the hands weave so that a fine, sturdy flaxen rope begins to emerge. The result contains the strength of each individual thread brought together into a powerful whole, and as well as being the sum strength of the threaded parts, there is a sense that the final product is of an even greater strength still thanks to the power of natural cohesion.

At first it may seem that we have much more work to do than the old Irish cottagers, for their flax had been handed to them by Mother Nature, whereas we are dealing in flax of a complicated, intellectual sort that we must hand to our own selves from the Naturescape of the mind. At the risk of flattering ourselves, it's tempting to say that, yes!- the philosophers in this case do indeed have a rougher challenge on their hands than the cottagers. But this said, we are actually getting off a good deal more lightly than we might have, and here's why...

When all is said and done, we will not have woven an actual rope of our own. Rather, we will have taken part in an ongoing process of rope-twisting, a process that has been in perpetual motion since at least as long ago as the days of the Ancient Greeks. Yes, we will be presenting an important thread of our own, and we will be twisting it into the rope's fabric, but other historical hands will be twining their respective threads in and out of ours, and the result will be a great cumulative effort.

The twisting of the first thread was commenced by the remarkable Ancient Greek writer Epicurus (c.341-270 BC). Epicurus was the first philosopher to truly see life and existence as being hinged around pleasure. In a world that is often terrible and frightening, the Epicureans resolved to embrace happiness, and endeavoured to live life to its fullest. Epicureanism encourages a wonderfully humane, positive philosophy. Happiness was seen to be a human being's raison d'etre, and a person's individual entitlement to happiness was extended in the philosophy towards others, so that the idea of 'happiness for all', rather than 'happiness at the expense of others', reigned supreme.

A wildness that might have so easily crept into a pleasure-cult like this was tempered in Epicureanism by a sense of morality that was both rational and dignified. Both one's personal health and one's harmony with others depended upon a controlled, non-gluttonous approach to pleasure, and this sort of what we might describe as rational dignity promoted a sense of moderation and a humane inclination towards all things pacifistic and non-hurtful, and, morally speaking, a leaning towards all things Good.

The student of the history of philosophy will encounter a vast amount of tortured souls who have taken it upon themselves to work their thoroughly grim views of life into myriad dark portrayals of philosophical pessimism. How remarkable that the voice of Epicurus can declaim the unadulterated pleasures of life so enduringly in the face of all this prevailing morbidity! When we find ourselves bogged down in the misery of Schopenhauer, who assures us that our existence is pointless, grim and terrible, and who warns us that the best thing we can do is to turn away from the world utterly for as long as we are forced to endure in it- when we find ourselves, we are saying, bogged down in all this misery, overwhelmed by the black Schopenhauerian side of the philosophical coin, we can take great solace in the knowledge that we can turn that coin of philosophy over and find a lighter side to it, and there, minted into the white metal, is the benevolent face of Epicurus.

Much of philosophy has been preoccupied with rational argument on the subject of pleasure. Epicurus's message seems to allow all these great complexities to fall away. Put simply, he acknowledges the truths put forward by the Schopenhauers of this world, namely, that life can be tough; but, however difficult the world may seem, he reminds us of the undeniable fact that we all, being human, have a remarkable capacity for pleasure. The onus is on us to make the decision to use this wonderful gift.

Epicurus has sounded a special key-note for us here, so before we greet the next pair of hands that take part in the twisting of our rope we will let that pleasant note ring out a few moments longer. As it does so, let's wander off the path of philosophy and into the Gardens of Art History for a page or two. Among the most pleasurable of these appealing gardens is the one devoted to an attitude to Art known as Aestheticism, and it is here that we lay ourselves down in the shade to gather in the scents of the flowers and the hues of the blossoms.

Aestheticism was the approach to Art that spawned the 'aesthetic movement', a name given to the popular movement that took root in some circles of the British and French Arts scene towards the latter part of the Nineteenth Century. The actual word 'aesthetics' comes from philosophy, and refers to philosophies associated with Art and with Beauty. Aestheticism was founded on the notion that Art shouldn't have to have a direct objective or foist a particular social message onto its audience; Art was held to be self-sufficient, and of and for its own self.

In the tradition of Epicurus, Aestheticism was absolutely in love with pleasure, and it associated the love of pleasure with the appreciation of the quality of Beauty. Nowhere did Beauty seem to be more abundant, more capable of invoking fabulous moods, more sublime, than in Art. When he looked into the world of Art the aesthete saw great and timeless Beauties that seemed to outlast the transience of the passing world around him. The Beautiful rose of the world fades and dies, but the

Beautiful rose of Art is forever young. And more than all this, Art seemed to transcend the often bleak and frightening realities of the real world itself. In a time of trouble Art had a power to move one's mind to greater things, or, as Oscar Wilde put it, it lifted man out of the 'gutter' of the real and into the fabulous world of the stars overhead. In Aestheticism, the pursuit of Beauty through Art became an important end in itself, just as for Epicurus the pursuit of pleasure was an end in its own self.

It is now well over a century since these perspectives on Art held proper currency, but if it is agreed that such thinking is 'wrong' nowadays, surely it has rarely seemed so right to be wrong. Who has stood before a painting approaching the power of the flaxen-haired image depicted in John Everett Millais's *The Bridesmaid* and failed to respond to the curious loveliness that it lays before its audience? Don't we find there an inexpressible power that strikes us, entertains us, inspires us for the sake of our own delight? Hasn't the *First Movement of Beethoven's Moonlight Sonata* captured the ears of its listeners since its notes first rang out? And are we so very wrong to suppose that this is because the quality of Beauty has been imprisoned in its notes, like some gentle, unknowable prehistoric creature preserved for all time in musical amber? Or when we read the poem *On the Nature of Things,* written by Lucretius in tribute to Epicurus himself, don't we find its verses spilling the secrets of pleasure into us, unbidden even, through the power of Beauty? Surely there is nothing too controversial in all this?!

Controversial or no, those associated with Aestheticism often found themselves in hot water, and this was primarily due to what we might describe as Aestheticism's cumulative pronouncements on Ethics. The crux of the contention was that aesthetes held that Art should be a sphere free of moral concerns. Let's take a quick look at what this entails.

Whereas a Priest might stress that a particular painting should carry a pious, moral message in line with what religious thinking says is right and wrong, or whilst a Politician might demand that a novel should reflect the political outlook of whatever empowered government he happens to be representing, the aesthetic school insists that an artist should be free to create artwork as he or she sees fit. Let's leave theology to the clergyman, says the aesthete, and politics to the politician, and let us leave Art to the expert in that respective area too, namely, the artist. Controversial as this idea may have been in Victorian times, surely our modern era might do well to learn something from this two-Centuries-old perspective- how tediously often do we find the familiar ream of busy-bodies queuing up to meddle in the work of artistic excellence!

Whilst the Victorian Priest was trafficking in the Bible that underlay Christian theology, literary English Aestheticism, in a purely artistic sense, was constructing its own Biblical history. Here we find Oscar Wilde casting himself in the role of a self-sacrificial Christ figure, Epicurus and Plotinus as the two major prophets of the Old Testament, Walter Pater as the Saint Paul of the New Testament, Aubrey Beardsley as a sort of Apocalyptic Saint John, John Ruskin and Arthur Symons as two lesser New Testament sages, and Ernest Dowson and Lionel Johnson as two evangelising psalm-writers; leaving the mainstream Victorian public, whose dull, coarse morality first elevated the movement before impinging upon it and ultimately destroying it, to conform to a sort of Judas type role.

As those influenced by Aestheticism looked around themselves and saw the passing of life, the hardships of the real world, and the difficulties that face all men and women, they realised that Art provided a sort of timeless realm, a realm where Beauty didn't decay, and where the Imagination could run free, creating and conjuring as many wonderful things as a given artist's mind had the capacity of genius to produce. It seemed, indeed, that the Priest and the Politician had it wrong: they said that Art should get in the queue behind life and be subservient to it; the aesthete felt that the dangerous, tiring, drudging real world should get in line behind Art, which was at once exciting, timeless, pleasurable and Beautiful. In reaching this singular conclusion Aestheticism had flipped conventional thinking on its head and inaugurated a vibrant new phase in Art: it was time for the Priest and the Politician to take a backseat and be lectured by the Artist for a change.

As a natural result of these things, Aestheticism became one of the only Art philosophies to have been actually lived in real life. The movement can be said to have consisted of aesthetic artists, aesthetic critics, and also, interestingly, actual 'aesthetes', who were usually affected 'arty' types that swung between, on the one hand, the thoroughly pretentious and, on the other, the thoroughly good fun. John and Algernon in Oscar Wilde's The Importance of Being Earnest are aesthetes par excellence, as is Henry Wotton in Oscar's novel *The Picture of Dorian Gray*. Oscar himself was the arch-aesthete in real life, by the time he was in his mid-twenties having lectured all over America and having gained the nickname 'The Professor of Aesthetics.' In poetry, Charles Baudelaire is exemplary of the movement, and in painting, Dante Gabriel Rossetti.

Anyhow, let's wander out of the Gardens of Art History and return to our rope so that we can see who will come along after Epicurus to help us in our twisting.

We find that the second thread is taken up by Plotinus (204-269AD), that great philosophical marker in the flow of Western thought between antiquity and the Christian-dominated medieval period.

ANCIENT PHILOSOPHY
- PLOTINUS -
CHRISTIAN PHILOSOPHY

The last of the great philosophers of antiquity, and of integral importance to the development of Christian philosophy, which was to rise up after his death and dominate Western thought until the time of the Renaissance, Plotinus was the founder of Neo-Platonism. As a follower of Plato, Plotinus was influenced by Plato's theory of Ideas and Forms, whereby an Idea such as Beauty was seen as having a transcendent existence that was independent of space and time, and everyday Forms, such as a tree or a mountain, were believed to be copies of an ideal tree or an ideal mountain existing outside of time and place. In keeping with this, Plotinus was dedicated to contemplation, for contemplation brought him into direct contact with the eternal world of Ideas.

He adored Imagination. His faith in the contemplation of Beauty and the transcendent themes and symbols of the intellect can be seen to parallel the contemplation of Beauty and symbol stimulated by the aesthete's contemplation of Art. "Consider," Plotinus wrote, "the case of pictures: those seeing by the bodily sense the productions of the art of painting do not see the one thing in the one only way; they are deeply stirred by recognizing in the object depicted to the eyes the presentation of what lies in the idea, and so are called to recollection of the truth - the very experience out of which Love rises."

As a follower of Plato, it is natural that Plotinus should have had a faith in the world of the ideal, for it is a fundamental part of Plato's teaching. It also, in the uncertain, war-riven days in which Plotinus lived, allowed human beings to transcend the hardships of reality by finding a kind of solace within themselves through the world of inner thought. What is much less natural, however, is Plotinus's deep, wonderful appreciation of the tangible, sensuous world around him. Not only was the material world a difficult place to be stuck in back in those days, but it was pervaded by philosophers who tended to take a pessimistic view of it all, such as the Gnostics, who held that the material world was inherently Evil. It is wonderful that Plotinus was able to resist the forces that could so easily have turned his work into some deathly system of bleakness, thereby depriving the human race of one of its greatest, most precious optimists.

Indeed, we have already highlighted the remarkable rise of Epicurean optimism in a history of Western philosophising that is often weighted down horribly by pessimism; however Epicureanism's rise to prominence in a more general social-historical context seems even more remarkable than its rise within the abstract history of philosophy. During Epicurus's lifetime warring was constant, human life was especially fragile, and there was no sense whatsoever of social security in the way that we know it today.

In the violent, pestilential time in which Epicurus lived, the decision to embrace the fundamental pleasures of existence was not merely laudable, it was heroic. We have contrasted him philosophically with the pessimism of Schopenhauer, and in this historical context too both philosophers may be contrasted, Schopenhauer having lived a much more comfortable life in comparison to Epicurus. It is, ironically, very likely that Schopenhauer lived a happier life than Epicurus did when all is said and done (due, I need hardly stress, to his comfortable circumstances, rather than any inherent superiority in his ethical philosophy); and this said, Schopenhauer comes across by comparison as one whose unhappiness and misery in his writings often seems a pitiful indulgence.

It is remarkable, then, that Plotinus should have been possessed of not only the great love he held for mankind, but of such a strong, overwhelming love for the sensuous world around him. Surely the man who wrote the following words held nothing but the deepest type of appreciation for the material world of the senses.

Who that truly perceives the harmony of the Intellectual Realm could fail, if he has any bent towards music, to answer to the harmony in sensible sounds? What geometrician or arithmetician could fail to take pleasure in the symmetries, correspondences and principles of order observed in visible thing...?

Now, if the sight of Beauty excellently reproduced upon a face hurries the mind to that other Sphere, surely no one seeing the loveliness lavish in the world of sense - this vast orderliness, the form which the stars even in their remoteness display - no-one could be so dull-witted, so immovable, as not to be carried by all this to recollection, and gripped by reverent awe in the thought of all this, so great, sprung from that greatness. Not to answer thus could only be to have neither fathomed this world nor had any vision of that other.

In historical terms Plotinus should be seen as nothing less than the great guardian of Imagination and Beauty. As we have said, he arrived at a time where he would act as a swinging door between the great philosophers of antiquity and the coming philosophies of Christianity. There is much in Christian philosophy to recommend itself to the causes that Epicurus and Plotinus exemplify - and the life of Saint Francis, it should be said, might be seen to embody a human life as it would be lived were it to be brought as close as possible to a sort of ethical perfection - but I cannot, in all honesty, find that Christianity at any stage lends itself towards the spinning of an actual thread for our rope.

Indeed, a slipping of our rope takes place after the time of Plotinus. Here, Bertrand Russell sums up the falling away:

> In its early form [Christianity] placed all good
> in the life beyond the grave, thus offering men a
> gospel which was the exact opposite of that of
> Epicurus...

There is in the mysticism of Plotinus nothing morose or hostile to beauty. But he is the last religious teacher, for many centuries, of whom this can be said. Beauty, and all the pleasures associated with it, come to glorify ugliness and dirt. Julian the Apostate, like contemporary orthodox Saints, boasted of the populousness of his beard. Of all this, there is nothing in Plotinus.

After Plotinus, Christian philosophy goes on to posit true Beauty and goodness as existing in a heavenly afterlife, whilst mankind, cast from God's Edenic side, is condemned to struggle through life in its fallen, sinful state in a bid to atone for inherent impurity. Amid all this we find the falling away of an Epicurian faith in the pleasures of life as we live it, and considerably less room is made for the Neo-Platonist's passion for our world's Beauty in the here and the now of the life that we lead on earth, be it of the intellectual or the sensual sort.

A turning from the world's Epicurian pleasures in favour of a new emphasis upon varying degrees of self-immolation, and the replacement of Plotinus's faith in the Beauty of forms and ideas with an emphasis on man as fallen and sinful, would sit only with difficulty among a Western civilisation that still, let it be remembered, inhabited the same earth that Plotinus and Epicurus walked before it, namely, a pleasure-filled, Beautiful one. 'Give me Chastity and Continence' Saint Augustine is heard asking God, 'only not yet'.

We must wait some time before the next thread of flax is taken up, and though the wait is a little excruciating, it is most definitely worth it in the end. Our destination is Benedict Spinoza (1632-1677), an exemplary scholar raised in Amsterdam who would distinguish himself as one of the foremost 'rationalists' in philosophy. We discussed earlier that when particular strands of Nineteenth Century thinking culminated in Aestheticism the result was the creation of one of the only philosophies in Art (and perhaps one of the few philosophies in general?) that would be genuinely lived by some of its adherents.

In Spinoza's case, we find a similarly rare example of a man who practiced what he preached and who lived a life reflecting his philosophical beliefs. In his philosophical worldview, for instance, money had no overwhelming importance in the great scheme of things, which is easily said, but not so easily practiced; Spinoza, however, put his money where his mouth was and lived a life that showed paltry regard for financial prosperity.

Spinoza was a 'pantheist', that is, he saw God as being present everywhere, both in all worldly things, and beyond all worldly things. René Descartes (1596-1650) had offered ingenious rational evidence in support of the definition of matter, or 'substance', as a phenomenon that requires nothing outside of itself to exist; but Spinoza saw that one object or thing is always connected or relational to another object or thing, and so from one matter or substance we are continually referencing out further and further.

To bring Descartes' judgment to its sensible conclusion, Spinoza realised, we must declare that the complete totality of everything is the only thing that must have nothing beyond itself. There is nothing outside of the totality of everything that one can possibly reference out to, and so this wholeness is a pantheistic completeness that we identify with God.

Descartes had also used fine rational argument to illustrate that God was an entity with no limits, and, again, Spinoza took the work of Descartes further, realising that God must consequently be present in all things if this thinking is to be brought to its logical conclusions. If God were absent in, say, non-human mammals, or plants, or forests, or mountains, he would therefore be limited, yet the logic of Descartes had illustrated God's unlimited nature.

For God to be limitless, God must be absolutely pervasive. Hence Spinoza's pantheism. In a world where he held a benevolent God to be present in all things at all times, it should come to us as no great wonder that Spinoza felt the loveliness of our existence deeply, and that he beheld the Beauty of the world in a special way. As an aesthete might express it, he saw divine Beauty everywhere.

So too Spinoza, the world that we inhabit is fundamentally Good, and this echoes the emphasis on the world's goodness that we have found in the joyous writings of Plotinus. Spinoza had a Jewish upbringing, but due to his independent thinking he found himself expelled from the Jewish community by the time of his mid twenties.

Conventional Jewish thinking tended to advise man to turn his back on pleasure, for pleasure, particularly of the sensuous variety, was frequently identified with sinfulness and Evil. Spinoza, however, perceived pleasure as a fundamental goodness, and in this he is refreshingly at one with Epicurus. He also had a favourable appreciation for one of the most natural human consequences of pleasure: emotion.

Unlike the many philosophers who argued that emotion was a negative, even repulsive human attribute (such as the Stoics), Spinoza saw the goodness in human emotion in a manner not dissimilar to the way in which he saw the goodness in pleasure. He disliked an emotion only when it spilled over into an irrational passion. We have often seen the negative, fanatical kind of passion that Spinoza warns us against guiding the speech of our more narrow-minded politicians in Northern Ireland.

This recalls our earlier reflections on Epicurus, where we touched on the dangerous idea of pleasure in an unbridled state, which is in no way dissimilar to Spinoza's admonitions against emotion in an unbridled state here. As with Epicurus, we find that a sense of rational dignity is desired where the worship of pleasure is concerned, be it of an emotional nature or otherwise. And so in cumulative considerations of the attitudes taken by Spinoza, Plotinus and Epicurus concerning pleasure, we find that a general stance begins to emerge: as long as a person retains a sense of rational dignity, and keeps a sensible, considerate head on his or her shoulders, the pleasure-seeker must be allowed to embrace life's joys without guilt, without hindrance, and with a great sense of delight.

In Plotinus, Epicurus, and Spinoza, we have discovered the three great threads of our rope into which our own thread must be twisted. There are, however, other people of note who, though they haven't contributed a thread themselves, or even come close to doing so, have donated some yarn, yarn that strengthens our rope greatly.

Chief amongst these is John Scotus Erigena (c.810-877), the great Irishman who lived at a time when the Roman Empire's civilized Europe had been crushed by Germanic tribes. In Western Europe the barbarians had taken Britain but had stopped short of Ireland, and so over the 6th-8th Centuries civilisation and learning amongst the Irish had continued relatively undisturbed.

Erigena followed Neo-Platonic thought as established by Plotinus, and worked it into his Christianity with the result that his philosophy became remarkable for an early kind of Christian rationalism. In projecting this sense of rationalism onto the Bible he came to see much of the text as allegorical. Believing creation to be timeless, he concluded that the Genesis account was an allegorical expression of creation rather than a literal one. Like Spinoza, Erigena was a pantheist.

He believed God to be a force of goodness that pervaded all things; and therefore, like Spinoza after him, there is a sense that Erigena felt the Beauty of the world over the badness of it, a badness that many pessimistic Christian contemporaries insisted on holding to be in a terrible ascendancy here on earth. Continuing his rationalist, humane interpretation of the Bible, he rejected the idea that the sinful are condemned to perpetual torment in Hell, and even believed that God, in his kindness and compassion, would forgive and reinstate the Devil himself.

In Erigena we find a refreshing mind that perceived the delight and Beauty of being alive, and one that was unafraid to transcend established Christian, philosophical, social and other restricting conventions of his time by the power of his own rational character. This resistance to systems, as we will see later, is integral to the rejuvenated Aestheticism we are geared towards in this booklet. Erigina's philosophical talents and sense of free-thinking elevate him as an Individual above many other fine minds that could not shake themselves similarly free from the ideological shackles of the Dark Ages.

One will discern little difference between Erigena's defiant free-thinking and the struggle to transcend social, political and moral systems on the part of the aesthete and artist in the history of Aestheticism.

Jeremy Bentham (1748-1832), one of the most outstanding Englishmen of all time and the founder of Utilitarianism, also lends important fibres to our rope.

His Utilitarian school was imbued with humanity and devoted to liberalism and the belief that a fundamental function of society should be to share a just and even grade of pleasure amongst all of its members. As we have seen, Epicurus argued that pleasure should be of central importance to human life, and it is perhaps Utilitarianism that has adapted his argument to the modern world in the most consciously practical way.

The Utilitarians defined pleasure as the absence of pain, and believed that society should be a collectively moral entity that should aim at doing the greatest amount of good for the greatest amount of people. This puts an onus on the collective political system to gear itself towards the betterment of mankind, but also on the Individual, who must make moral choices and be responsible for the consequences his or her actions will have for others.

And less significant to our rope than Bentham's school, though influential nonetheless, is Jean-Jacques Rousseau (1712-1778), the Swiss writer who went some way towards generating the Romantic school in Art. Rousseau reinstated the importance of man's subjectivity and sense of emotion in human values at a time when the cold, unfeeling logic espoused by the rise of science and the Enlightenment had done a lot to stamp it out, and because of this he is of importance to the artist, for emotion is an integral colour on the palate of artistic creation. In the Art favoured by Aestheticism, indeed, Rousseau's heightened emotion has the opportunity to run to a fever-pitch, to very insanity itself, and the Art in question can be the more brilliant for it.

The latter stages of this booklet, for reasons that will become apparent, will be recommending a return to the sort of Rousseau-esque emotion in Art that evokes great, sweeping passion. But beyond the world of Art, in the reality of Life, the more crazed aspects of Rousseau's emotion theory can be irreparably damaging, and we are reminded of Spinoza's warning that emotion is one of life's great goodnesses only until the moment that it spills over into uncontrolled passion.

Such passions, untempered by what we have described as rational dignity, have caused some of the worst atrocities in history, from the most heinous acts of the Nazis, to the mindless 'hate' crimes we're accustomed to hearing about on the news every week.

We're left, after all this is said and done, with a rope that gains its strength of character through several important convictions. Firstly, the world is Good, and human existence itself is a type of goodness. Secondly, Beauty is central to existence, and the appreciation of pleasure is a chief purpose in life. Thirdly, we have a moral obligation to try and do what will have the best possible outcome for those who are affected by our actions, which means that a pleasure-thirst should be tempered by the common-sense moral considerateness we've described as rational dignity.

In having tightened up these threads in our important rope we have simultaneously started to unfurl the carpet of what can be called New Aestheticism, and as we begin to walk down this carpet now, our first few footfalls take us into the realms of the creative Imagination.

On Ethics

Thomas L. Muinzer

THE CREATIVE IMAGINATION

Even if we allow only for the crucial role that imaginativity plays in Art, it is impossible to deny that the human Imagination is amongst the utmost of human powers. In Art the Imagination creates entire worlds never before witnessed, furnishes these worlds with strange peoples, wild creatures, unreal happenings and curious perceptions. When a person steps into the mantle of 'artist' he or she comes as close as ever a person can to becoming a God, for it is only in this guise that man can create entire worlds at a whim. Indeed, the Imagination of the artist at its height can seem so powerful that it would appear to transcend the very forms that constitute its boundaries.

Let's consider, for instance, that special imaginative fire called upon by the combined poetic genius of Wordsworth, Coleridge, and Keats, three poets identified with England's Romantic school, a movement intensely concerned with emotion, a la Rousseau. Even taken alone, these three poets have imaginatively pushed the limits of emotion in their work to such a height that to the reader, at times, it seems as if they have literally invented new kinds of feelings in their work.

If a logical, unimpulsive cold-fish of a person was to submerge himself in the work of these poets intensely enough and with a mind suitably open to new experience, it would not be at all remarkable that a sort of osmosis might start to occur between him and the poetry, that our friend's feelings might start to become richer, that his moods might become more curious and Beautiful. It's almost as if, he might think to himself in that dull-headed, logical way of his, the Romantic feelings have transcended the art-form that bounds them and have entered into me! To the aesthete's sensitive mind this seeping of Art into life would seem scarcely remarkable.

It might seem less surprising than it sounds, then, if we are reminded that the great liberal John Stuart Mill claimed his political sympathies were brought into line with Socialism and the plight of the working class as he got older due to his reading of the Romantic poets.

Yes, few will venture to deny that the Imagination is amongst the most integral of human ingredients in Art. But who also can venture to deny that the Imagination ranges infinitely far beyond the realm of Art?- in conversation, how frequently do we find the human Imagination dragging our dialogue into strange territories that rational logic could never possibly divine; and how often do we see children weaving a world of 'make-believe' in their games, games that can proceed so entirely from the Imagination that they may seem completely incomprehensible to onlooking adults; and as for our idea of that loose concept we call 'culture' - well, let's stop there, for when dealing with our culture it would nearly be easier to list what Imagination has not generated than what it has.

Culture is nothing more than a great jigsaw, and the concrete pieces of the jigsaw - things like ritual events, or particular human interests - have been coloured in by the richness of the creative human Imagination itself. Indeed, so much of what we understand to be culture is so closely associated with the domain of the human Imagination that a sense of culture in itself is little more than a great concretising of Imaginative human psychology.

Let's take the subject of taste, for instance. For argument sake we will put it in the context of the world of fashion (in Western culture). It will not be surprising to find that a girl from Belfast will share a sense of what is acceptable as 'excellent' taste with other Western girls from other Western cities, because they also partake of what we loosely call Western culture; so a girl from Bologna, or London, or Boston, will be on a similar wavelength to our hypothetical Belfast belle if she, too, is in any way keeping up with her modern cultural trends.

Is it an appeal to logic that makes us favour current Western tastes in fashion over, say, the supposedly civilised Western tastes of a couple of hundred years ago?

It's surely not logic, for the marked changes in taste that history offers us are hardly entirely rational changes. '2 + 2 = 4' is more rational than '2 + 2 = 5', but it is not more rational to prefer baseball caps to the Victorian bowler in the way that we do today. Could it be an appeal to emotion that dictates our sense of taste then?- can we here in the UK pinpoint anything markedly less emotionally rewarding in having the gentlemanly ruff from

Elizabethan times around our necks instead of the modern dressy shirt collar? Surely not.

Maybe, then, fashion taste is merely the result of the outright aesthetic appeal of clothing? We might find evidence to support this idea through the analogy of music, whereby particular chords are classed as 'concords' and others are classed as 'discords', the former sounding naturally pleasant to the human ear, the latter sounding naturally unpleasant. Maybe certain kinds of fashion are naturally 'concordant' and others are naturally 'discordant', and so our sense of taste is formed by our innate responses to what we hold naturally to be attractive and unattractive.

It is hard to deny that this is partly the case; however fashion taste is always in flux, simultaneously coming and going, and what we hold to be attractive in dress now will no doubt be held to be horrendously unfashionable in a couple of centuries time (if not in a couple of days time!). So we cannot properly reconcile our cultural perceptions of what constitutes good taste in fashion here with the innate aesthetic concordance we sometimes observe elsewhere, as in music.

Being neither wholly logical, emotional, nor innately concordant, fashion taste, therefore, makes its strongest appeal to the imaginative domains of human psychology. We do not find independent laws pre-existing in reality to instruct us in the construction of our fashion sense; rather, we journey within, and create the fluctuating laws of fashion through internal imaginativity. In the sense that we take it here, 'taste' in fashion is little more than an imaginative human construct in itself.

But fashion is merely one example; the same can easily be said for many other, non-fashion related dimensions of taste, and, beyond that, of many other areas we commonly identify as constituting our 'culture' in general.

So perhaps the role that the Imagination plays in our everyday world is less simplistic than many suppose. Most would take it as a given that the Imagination can create worlds in an 'artistic' sense, in the way that, say, Jonathan Swift's Imagination has created the worlds visited by Gulliver in his *Gulliver's Travels*. Yet the Imaginative realm of the artist is generally held to be very distinct from the real world around us, from the world as we actually find it. Surely, most people assume, reality in itself embodies the world in which we exist, and Imagination, if it may have any real bearing on these things at all, offers us a retreat from this reality, in the way that we might open *Gulliver's Travels* for a bit of, as it's called, 'escapism'.

Yet our musings on the relevance of the Imagination to culture have been seen to disturb this comfortable view of life and Art a little. And rightly so, for there is a rupture between the boundary dividing the real world in which we live from the world of the Imagination. Let's take an example in order to expose this rupture, a particularly Irish example for which purpose I will be introducing the reader to a couple of new friends, David and Jiang...

Two international schools have set up a pen-pal program for their pupils, and from a young age David, from Belfast, and Jiang, from Beijing, have been exchanging letters. Through their correspondence they become good friends, and they keep their writing up even after they've finished primary school. As soon as their parents feel they are old enough, it is decided that David will head to China for a holiday, where he will stay with Jiang's family in Beijing, and after two weeks Jiang will fly back with David and stay for a while with his family in Belfast.

Though still just a young lad, David has already heard many of the famous stories about the Great Wall of China - that it's the longest man-made structure in the world, that it's rumoured to be the only man-made feature on earth that can be seen from the moon, etc. He has also heard the Wall mentioned in Jiang's letters, Jiang having made several references to this proud part of his cultural heritage. Though young David hasn't seen so much as a picture of the Great Wall before, these things have given him a pretty good idea of what it will be like, and he is very excited about visiting it. Once he reaches China, Jiang's family happily agree to take David on a day trip to the Wall, and the boys have a fun time exploring it, climbing it, walking on its pathway, and a bystander even takes a few great photos of the pair of them standing in front of it.

After the holiday David returns to Belfast and brings Jiang with him. Jiang himself has heard famous things about a sort of 'Great Wall' in Northern Ireland, the stories of which have travelled around the world just like the stories about the Great Wall of China. He has also heard about it in David's letters, the subject having cropped up every so often as an important part of David's sense of his culture. Indeed, Jiang learns that David's family are Irish Republicans, and that the Wall has special significance regarding their cultural self-perception. The 'Wall' in question here is more commonly referred to as the North/South Irish border, and Jiang, of course, is as eager to see it as David was to see the Great Wall of China.

Like David with the Chinese Great Wall, newly-arrived Jiang has a similar set of references and pre-conceived notions concerning the Northern Irish border, and has, in fact, a literal image of what it must be like in his mind, though he has seen no pictures of it.

As soon as he arrives, indeed, he is already hearing the lifestyle in Northern Ireland being contrasted to the lives of those 'below the border' and 'down South'. All this considered, it's surely no wonder that Jiang is as keen to see the Great Border as David was to see the Great Wall. It is only with the greatest of difficulty that David's parents are able to explain to him that he would be visiting a kind of nothingness if he paid a visit to it. This is difficult for Jiang to grasp. Why?

Jiang knows that this supposed barrier is of utmost historical and ideological significance to Ireland's heritage, and loosely grasps that it is the great divider separating two varied economies, two different governments, two contrasting cultural and civic systems on the single island of Ireland. He has the difficult mental task of reconciling his own preconceptions and issues like these with reality in a way that David did not have in the Great Wall of China's case. David's parents make clear to him that, if he were to visit the famous border, he would find, merely, a continuous fluid landscape flowing between the North and the South of Ireland. At best, there might be a border patrol of police, or a checkpoint of sorts, though there probably wouldn't even be that; and there certainly wouldn't be a physical feature like a ring of mountains dividing the North from the South, or even so much as a man-made wire fence. There is no Great Wall that can be seen or touched in order to build upon the mind's psychological pre-understanding.

As the young boy's mind tries to correlate this curious information with its preconceptions, one can forgive Jiang for asking David's parents where the border actually exists if there is, in truth, no border actually there for him to go and visit. We can also forgive Jiang if the answers he receives seem strangely unsatisfactory. 'We are told it exists by politicians, so that's one way it exists' the parents say. 'It's written about a lot in history books and newspapers, so it exists in those places as well.' 'Plus it's on maps. And people talk about it, and it's in the news. It exists in those places too.'

If these answers seem unsatisfactory to our young friend it is for the simple reason that they are easily demolished. 'We are told it exists by politicians, so that's one way it exists'; and if we're told by politicians that pigs can fly, does that make it so? 'It's on maps'; and Jiang might, as many have done before him, produce a map of Atlantis, and so, then, has he verified the existence of Atlantis? 'People talk about it'; and people also talk about unicorns and so, therefore, do unicorns exist? 'It's in the news'; and if the news tells us that a Queen's University Professor has discovered the secret of immortality, do we take the story for fact? Neither flying pigs, Atlantis, unicorns, nor (so far as I know) immortal Queen's Professors can be said with any certainty to exist.

The parents might have tried another angle by likening the border to the Chinese border, which divides the Chinese from the Russians, the Mongolians, the Nepalese, and so on. Being Irish Republicans, however, what might normally have been an intelligible comparison falls asunder, for the parents are of the conviction that they are every bit as 'Irish' as the people living below the border. Were the family Loyalist, they might argue the opposite, that the border makes them every bit as British as the rest of the British Empire.

Either way, the border, it would seem, does not divide nationalities in the way a conventional border does. Indeed, David's family confuse our young friend on this point further by going to some length to stress that he is currently in Northern Ireland, and that below the border he will find the South of / Republic of Ireland, and that there is merely one nation and one island, and that it is... Ireland. Consequently, Jiang, being a bright lad, comes to realise that, in the case of those possessed of a Republican mindset at any rate, the border actually strengthens a sense of shared Irish identity by emphasising the perceived threat that the very same border actually poses to Irishness.

Jiang is still left, therefore, with the following conundrum: where does the N.Irish border exist? It must be somewhere, for what Northern Irish person would deny, after all is said and done, that in its own way the North/South border is every bit as real as the Great Wall of China?

The answer I would suggest is that it exists in a sort of collective political Imagination.

This political Imagination interacts with all of the previously mentioned phenomena (visual representations such as maps, historical literature, media reports, everyday discourse, etc.), but it is still distinct in and of itself. The political Imagination describes a sort of mental space that not only allows us to receive knowledge of a sort of 'unreal reality', such as our intangible border, but that allows us to perpetuate such unreal realities by our decision to mentally accept them as real. Put crudely, the North/South border is a figment of the Imagination...

...albeit a very real figment.

When the brevity of reality rings true for the human race and the whole lot of us have been buried by nuclear explosion, or by great sweeping plagues, and the barren earth becomes the domain of the scuttling cockroach, what can all this mean for the Walls of David and Jiang? With the erasure of humankind comes the erasure of those things that generated the North/South border; social discourse, cultural ideology, and all the other abstractions that come together into a solid Great Wall within the political Imagination of the human mind. For the scuttling cockroach racing across the post-human earth, no Irish border will obstruct him. As to his cockroach cousins in China, however, they will have found something to nest in, and to clamber upon. They will have found a Great Wall that will be wholly, undeniably there.

The human Imagination as we see it here is a far cry from something that is reserved for 'arty-farty' types, or for kids playing their imaginary games; it's an important mental device that both relays, and creates, our surrounding world. We can easily accept that Swift has created the world of Gulliver's Travels through the force of his Imagination, but is that process really so different to the process whereby a collective series of human minds bestow existence on an intangible North/South border? It would seem not.

An important marker in the development of man's understanding of the human Imagination arrived in the Seventeenth Century with René Descartes, the French rationalist philosopher and great predecessor of Spinoza. Descartes summed up an important part of his studies on the subject of what we can know of our own existence in the phrase *cogito ergo sum*, 'I think therefore I am'.

Here Descartes suggests that the most reliable yardstick we have in the pursuit of knowledge is our internal world of thought, as opposed to the world that we experience externally around us. Decartes' cogito makes the foundation of understanding different for each person, since the departure-point of interpretation is one's own self and since every single person is a unique, different person.

Developing this in the context of the Imagination, we can say with an unabashed sense of conviction that our Imagination resides within each one of us, as opposed to being something free-floating and external. Since it is within the Individual person that the Imagination resides, and since each Individual is unique, we can begin to broaden our thesis outward a little now towards consideration of the idea of the Individual itself.

THE INDIVIDUAL

When we arrive at the concept of 'the Individual', at the notion that each human being is diverse and unique, that each person is an entire world unto one's own self, we suddenly find that we begin to lose our grip on much of the unconscious faith we had in systems. Systems are the great generalisers of Western thought; and since each Individual is complex and diverse, we are continually reminded, therefore, of the great inadequacies that are part and parcel of all systems. Systems can be very helpful, and are, indeed, vital to civilised life, but they are also in the unwavering habit of robbing us of much more truth than they reveal as they generalise infinite variety into minute, finite categories.

Karl Marx tells us that he can explain away the whole of society with a Marxist 'superstructure' system based on working class, middle class, upper class, and that this somehow expresses all sectors of modern society. Gender theorists have seen fit to package our race continually into a two-part gender system, that of the male and female, and have implied that these two great categories can sum us all up and explain us all away - hey presto - just like that. To post-colonialist writers, race and skin colour underlie the explaining system; to others again, such as the 'Queer Theorists', the system takes the form of sexual orientation; and so on, and so forth. If each person is an infinitely complex Individual in his or her own right, to generalise in such ways on the subject of even one Individual is to dumb down a great vastness. When such generalisations are applied to more than one Individual at a time, we go beyond a mere dumbing down and enter the realms of absurdity.

Well!... perhaps 'absurdity' is being a little harsh on many of the great men and women who have contributed to systems like the ones mentioned here. And, besides, hasn't the world of literature given us the likes of Franz Kafka, who reminds us in his own absurd writing that 'absurdity' itself often has great value? Wisdom and Absurdity may be strange bedfellows, but they do have a habit of enjoying each other's company. But this doesn't mean the problems don't stand.
Ideas such as Marxism are associated with 'theory', that is to say, they are systematic statements of general principles, or, put another basic way, they are systems of thought. Much of the difficulty surrounding theory, particularly modern theory, stems

from the fact that theorists have not yet learned a hard lesson: the person who can generalise great sweeping laws that will explain away society does not exist, has never existed, and can never exist. The modern evolution of Marxism serves to emphasise the point.

The influential modern Marxist Louis Althusser, for instance, has watered down Marxist conceptions of economic determinism and called the result overdeterminism; he has diluted the Marxist connection between culture and economics in his theory of relative autonomy; he has loosened the precedence given to economics in Marx's conception of the 'superstructure'. But is all this really a 'development' of Marxism, or merely a concession to the failings of a totalising and therefore flawed theoretical system? Even the most devoted Althusserian would find it hard to deny that, as he sets about expanding Marxism out in sensible directions, Althusser, little bit by little bit, becomes increasingly un-Marxist in his pronouncements.

Consequently the problematic nature of theoretical systems presents us with an important question: does the infinite unfathomableness of a single Individual, let alone a whole cross-section of our race, therefore spell the death of theory?

No! Certainly not.

But it demands that theorists acknowledge that their own, often ingenious discoveries, are not totalising. The next great sweeping theoretical discoveries - and who can doubt that we have many more ahead of us - should be trumpeted with the natural sense of excitement that accompanies such things, but also with a sense of humility: "No, this is not the ultimate explanation of existence. But it is perhaps the most advanced understanding we have been able to present of our condition as a human race to date, and here are the reasons why..."
Further to this humility, a sense of compromise will also no doubt be called for. A few paragraphs previously we touched upon theoretical trends from literary, artistic and general philosophical studies that have all purported at one time or another to provide a sort of ultimate template for the interpretation of our world. Indubitably, Marxism, gender theory, post-colonialism, gay and lesbian theory (etc.) are all

independently wrong. In reality, a sort of compromise, in the context of these ideas at any rate, is probably ideal: class, gender, race, sexuality, and so forth, all have a place in our understandings of our modern condition. Certainly, no approach is entirely right, and therefore, used in a totalising way, each approach is entirely wrong.

A lack of compromise, indeed, has the tendency to damage excellent discoveries. We see a prominent example of this with the linguist Ferdinand de Saussure (1857-1913), the man who set the tone for modern theory and philosophy. Saussure realised that: language is arbitrary (words have no inherent meaning); a word is always defined off its relation to another word; language actually gives meaning to a thing it describes (because there is no inherent meaning actually contained in the things that language refers to). Perhaps his most famous saying is that 'in a language there are only differences, without fixed terms.'

These insights led Saussurean philosophy to the idea that language, and our world as language figures it forth, is based upon a state of pure difference. To the sensible mind the pushing of Saussure's fine ideas to such an extreme should seem flawed and illogical. The Saussurean errors here are generated by a classic lack of compromise; there must clearly be a compromise between language and the objectivities it refers to. The idea of difference is an important one, but it cannot be said we have merely pure difference and nothing besides, we must have differences between one thing and another thing.

Hence, compromise.

In the case of the Individual, then, to see him/her as merely a product of society, as Marxists for instance tend to have us believe, is to put the cart before the horse. The Individual is part of a social system, yes!; but the collective Individuals that constitute that very system are what create and sustain it. Moreover, as we have discussed, an important aspect of the human being that creates and sustains the system is the Imagination, and it should be remembered that the Imagination is an area that is considerably more subjective than it is objective.

So then, are we really constituted by socialisation, as is contended by most theorists? ['Socialisation'- a sort of way of expressing how a person automatically and unknowingly adopts the behaviour patterns of the culture he or she grows up in. TLM] The answer is, naturally, 'yes, of course.' It has been theorised, demonstrated, and proven beyond rational doubt. But here we recall the lessons of humility and compromise that intellectual history has taught us by now, and we recognise that the internal world of the Individual and the external world of society are both in operation and interaction.

We will also remember that the Individual is both objective and subjective. Even a cursory glance at the life and times of John Scotus Erigena, who we have rightly acknowledged in our rope twisting, makes it clear that the many fascinating things that emerged in his philosophy proceeded from his particularly stubborn, free-thinking attitude. It was this resolve to think freely and rationally, thereby going against the grain of the prevalent thought systems of his day, that made Erigena great. And he was by no means the only great Irishman to lend fibres to our rope in such a system-resisting manner: Oscar Wilde's efforts to transcend social and political concerns through Art as characterised by his place as the figurehead of Aestheticism can be seen to come from the same system-resistant tradition.

And we discover that this area of the age-old legacy of philosophy is bolstered by the more recent ascendancy of modern science. Science in essence is based upon the notion that there is an objective world external to man, and that this objective world can be observed, tested and measured scientifically, and that from our scientific observations we can learn more about how the world around us works.

The greatest scientist of the last century, Albert Einstein, revolutionised modern scientific understanding with his Theory of General Relativity. General Relativity reorganised human understandings of space and time by presenting them in the form of four-dimensional 'space-time', and bound up with this was the contention that space-time itself was curved. General Relativity was already supported by certain observable scientific facts when Einstein put it forward in 1915, and it was soon confirmed by further scientific and mathematic testing.

The space-time concept shows that absolute time (that is, linear time in the normal sense that people have generally understood it) doesn't exist. Instead, every Individual person has his or her own particular time that relates to his physical position and to the way in which he or she is moving, and when a body acts or exerts a force it actually affects the curvature of space-time itself.

In fact, physics has shown that if Person A is an astronaut who is zipping about in a spacecraft at the speed of light in the far-flung reaches of the galaxy, and if Person B, a friend of the astronaut and of an identical age to him, remains on Earth and goes about a normal life, time will act upon Person A to a lesser extent than it will act upon Person B. Indeed, with the correct time-space conditions in place, Person A could come back to Earth as a young man full of energy and in his prime only to be greeted by an old, wizened Person B that has aged far more quickly and is now all but unrecognisable to him.

Pretty amazing, but scientifically sound! Putting these things in the context of some of the philosophical and literary issues we're considering here, we find in all this that modern science is actually presenting time and space as two partially subjective phenomena. Philosophically speaking, Einstein's space-time concept displays an extreme subjectivity in that its laws mean that every subject, every Individual, has a particular and personal relation to the supposedly objective world outside of him or her self. It is in this sense that, even in the realms of furthest objectivity - the very fabric of the space-time dimensions that figure forth the objective world around us - the subject may be seen to have a greater power and influence than many of us might realize. In philosophy, Immanuel Kant had summed up such subjectivism with great insight before Einstein had even been born: "If we take away the subject space and time disappear: these as phenomena cannot exist in themselves but only in us."

"But hold on!" the Arts theorist cries after mulling over the idea of the Individual as being simultaneously subjective and objective; "the Individual is bitten and shaped internally by the very external world itself." ("We see that," he might add if he's in a wordy mood, "through Gramsci's theory of hegemony, or Foucault's discourses, or Althusser's interpellation.")

This is true, but on what ground can it be denied that the external world is also bitten and shaped from the inside out by the Individuals that create it? Every Individual co-constitutes the system, is an integral piece in its jigsaw. Each Individual is a miniature version of Tolkien's Gandalf, simultaneously conjuring society into being whilst allowing it to endure.

Just as each Individual is a little metaphorical Gandalf, and that this can be said to be a constant attribute shared generally amongst human beings, there are other, more concrete features of the human condition that appear to remain relatively constant too. Sensible observations will remind us that civilisation has taken many different forms (geographically, socially and historically speaking), and that many things in the human condition have transcended those forms across all times and cultures. Intellectually, an obvious example is the innate faith that various cultures invariably display in God(s). Even in the supposedly hyper-logical, secular Western world of our present day we find numerous people, even those topmost in the scientific and mathematic professions, expressing unshakable 'faith' (an utterly irrational concept) in the belief of (for example) the Christian conception of God.

In addition to intellectual examples, we will find numerous physical examples to add to our conception of human qualities that transcend social and historical context. Take the sensation of 'pain' for instance. If I were to take a short trip back in time to pay a visit to Louis Althusser (1918-1990) and I were to give him a hardy poke in the eye with my pen, I wouldn't be in the least bit surprised if it hurt him. It would hurt him as much, I dare say, as it would hurt Karl Marx (1818-1883) if I went a little further back and treated his eyeball to a similar jab. If Marx jabbed me back, as he'd have a fair right to do after my mistreatment, I'd feel pain too. Indeed, I could go back further again and jab Schopenhauer's eye for all it mattered, for the result would still be the same: pain. Pain is one of the most immediate examples of a physical human quality that has continually transcended social and historical context, and a whole intellectual shield of interpellation theory won't save the eyeballs of modern French Marxism from feeling its sting.

The intellectual and physical aspects encapsulated in the Individual that have remained relatively constant across diverse social and historical contexts illustrate that there are certain dimensions of man that no amount of social or cultural conditioning has yet been able to impinge upon in any truly deep way. Social systems themselves, however, are radically less constant; and if it comes to a head, it is, one may say at the very least, 'possible' to mount a convincing argument in favour of the contention that the Individual feeds the system more strongly than the system feeds the Individual. Surely modern theorists turn a blind eye to the existence of such an argument at their own work's peril.

If we had to sum these things up in a terse way, we could do so as follows: the more finely a logical system attempts to condense our race, and the more it claims to explain it, the narrower its parameters are, and the narrower its parameters are, the more the diversity of the Individual is lost, and, therefore, the more totalising a system is, the more ideologically false it is. It should be added that in various circumstances a totalising system may be more useful to us than one that is not, but its degrees of philosophical falsity are not disturbed by its degrees of usefulness.

We have acknowledged that each Individual contains an Imagination, and that each Individual is unique, but we have also touched upon the fact that the Individual is both subjective and objective, and it is this that takes us into the next stage of our discussions.

BINARY OPPOSITION

The idea of Subjective/Objective flow between the Individual and the social world he or she both constructs and is acted upon by sets up what is sometimes called a binary opposition. (These oppositions parallel what Roland Barthes describes as the symbolic code in his writings.) In the case of the 'subjective' and the 'objective' we find two direct opposites being expressed; and that there are 'two' of them and that they are 'opposite' gives rise to the terms binary and opposition respectively.

Our general understandings of our world are predicated upon binary opposition in one way or another, and life itself is little more than the mergence of varying twin polarities, which form a sort of tension of opposites that pull us this way and that way. Binaries help us to arrange our existence in a manner that is intelligible to us, and they give us a structure with which we can grasp the world. We can easily pluck examples out of the air of the sorts of binaries that allow us to build up our picture of the fundamentals of existence, including the 'Subjective/Objective' example already mentioned, and, e.g., Alive/Dead, Male/Female, Hot/Cold, High/Low, Fact/Fiction, Day/Night, etc., etc.

Both of the two terms in a binary opposition are co-dependent. In the case of the 'Alive/Dead' example, it is apparent that one state cannot exist without its direct opposite also existing, so that if there is no such thing as being 'Alive', there can be no conceivable state of being 'Dead', life and death being defined off of one another. Put another way, and taking 'Fact/Fiction' as a fresh example, one might as easily define 'Fact' as 'not Fiction', and 'Fiction' as 'not Fact', both terms in the binary being mutually co-dependent and relational concepts. A binary opposition, we can clearly see, is a sort of unified, contradictory whole.

And once again, recourse to modern science emphasises the fact that we are not merely dealing in airy-fairy philosophical abstractions here. In quantum mechanics, the highly influential set of revolutionary findings developed by some of the Twentieth Century's leading physicists (and including the aforementioned Albert Einstein), modern science has discovered that it is impossible to pinpoint both the position and the speed of particles at the same time. This has led experts towards the conception of quantum 'dualism', which now underlies our scientific understanding of the physical world. Quantum dualism is based around a Wave/Particle binary: applying their experimental findings to light waves, scientists have concluded that light waves must be conceived of as both waves and particles simultaneously.

The 'imaginative Individual', which has so far been the focus of our discussions, exists, we may say, within a world hinged around binary opposition. And so let us come to the most important opposition where the ethical life of each person is concerned, that of Good/Evil.

As far back in time as the Sixth Century BC, a time when philosophical development had supposedly barely begun, a Persian prophet had already perceived the supreme rootedness of the Good/Evil binary in man's existence. Zoroaster declared that human existence is the expression of an ethical conflict of Good against Evil, that man is irrevocably and inescapably bound up in this struggle, and that the conflict finds its purest expression through man's moral choices and deeds. And who can yet deny that there is an ingenious perceptiveness to this ancient insight? Time has proved Zoroaster right, for even today, centuries on, we find this notion of the struggle between Good and Evil underlying our lives. Every single moral choice we make swings a needle on the dial of Good/Evil towards one of its two extremities, and our entire moral existence is in some way touched on by the needle's tip as it shivers eternally between the polarities.

But if only things were that simple. The waters run more deeply than they might seem.

We know that both poles of a binary opposition are co-dependent upon one another for their very existence, and the binary of Good/Evil is no different. Good and Evil are a kind of unified whole. Pure goodness, that is, perfect goodness that accommodates no existence of any kind of contrary Evil whatsoever, is impossible; for pure goodness to exist there must be somewhere, somehow, the existence of an evilness against which the goodness can be defined.

Let us try and imagine how our current society might look if it was pervaded by pure moral Good, and let us imagine that Evil is non-existent. How far, I wonder, can we stretch such a conceit? Let us say that in our new world everyone gives as much change as they can spare to charity each day, everyone spends what free time they have engaged in actively helping others, everyone is as kind and conscientious as can be.

Due to what was briefly described as the 'relational' aspect of binaries, it is an unfortunate truth that a world like this cannot endure. Let's take a very mundane, every-day example to illustrate the untenable nature of our utopian vision, and imagine that we are having a meal at a restaurant. It is the convention at restaurants in this new version of our world, extremely benevolent and considerate as everybody now is, for the waiter to receive a whopping thirty-pound tip from each diner.

Very good of you, sirs! the lucky waiter thinks, no doubt, as we tip him.

But in fact, the waiter does not think this. In a world where a waiter continually receives a thirty-pound tip per head, we have not, strictly speaking, done an active goodness; we have made an 'average' gesture, which to the waiter is merely 'normal'. For a tip in this world of goodness to register in the waiter's head as being a truly significant act of goodness, the diner must make an active effort to be generous, thereby breaking the ritual of what is considered an average moral gesture.

Sixty pounds sir?! How very kind of you thinks the lucky waiter. But what of that table of misers who each only threw in a twenty pound tip?

What cheapskates! How mean! thinks the unlucky waiter.
(I need hardly remark that a twenty pound tip per head in our own culture would be considered very generous indeed!)

Hence, we see clearly how moral conceptions of goodness and badness are interlinked, and how each term helps regulate the other term depending on the context. In the world in which we all currently live, it is a good deed to wash your neighbour's car for him. In a world where everyone washes their neighbour's car, such as the perfect world we have just tried to envisage, it is a morally average deed to wash it, a bad deed not to wash it, and a good deed to go the extra mile and varnish it after the wash. However we put it, we find that goodness and badness are relational.

So we are in rather a quandary, and we can bring in Christian theology at this point to illustrate our dilemma. Moral questions frequently asked of God by Christians tend to take a form akin to the following:

"Why does God let bad things happen if he is naturally Good?"
or
"If God is Good then why does he allow Evil to exist?"

At first questions like these might seem impenetrable, however they can be solved by the binary logic we have explored above. We can express the binary solution to questions like these as follows:

'Good and Evil are mutually co-dependent, each respective term relying upon its own opposite in order for it to exist. Without the existence of moral Evil, moral Good itself cannot exist. If God had created a world free of Evil, therefore, he would also have created a world devoid of Good.'

But now we must develop our findings, and from here we enter the realms of a much deeper Christian dilemma: in creating a world of goodness, God necessarily created the simultaneous existence of Evil, and he also, therefore, created man's necessary capacity, if not propensity, for Evil. We may add to this that, since God knows and sees all, God knew that Adam and Eve would be tempted, that the apple would be eaten, and that man would Fall into Sinfulness and be cast from Eden. God foresaw it all, God knew it all, and yet he said let it be so.

Once out of the Garden, what sort of a moral world do the Fallen Adam and Eve find themselves in? They find themselves in a world structured around concepts of goodness, but in a world that is also inescapably defined off of evilness. It is Good to take in the starved, abused and homeless orphan, to nurture him and care for him with one's own love and at one's own expense; yet such generosity, the very opportunity to do this Good, has arisen by Evil; the murderer that took the life of the orphan's parents, the cruelty of a world that deprived him of a ready source of food, the malevolent steward who harassed him in the orphanage till he ran out alone into the cold world. Good and Evil, Evil and Good, no one without the other.

It is difficult, however, to conceive of a human world that could be anything but hinged on this Good/Evil binary. One possibility would be a world of indifference (though I do not pretend this would be a commendable alternative). An indifferent existence of this sort would appear to be glimpsed in the animal kingdom - or, at least, in our own human perceptions of the animal kingdom - where one does not 'blame' the leopard for hunting and consuming its prey; rather, the action is accepted with a type of moral indifference whereby it is seen to be inapplicable to or outside of the ethics of the Good/Evil binary. The leopard is neither Good nor Evil, it is merely natural.

We are reminded here of the passage from *The Critique of Pure Reason* where its author, the German philosopher Immanuel Kant (1724 - 1804), discusses the idea of human will. He observes that humans frequently feel that they ought to do particular things, whilst this moralistic compulsion does not appear in non-human nature. "The words I ought", he writes, "express a species of necessity, and imply a connection with grounds, which nature does not and cannot present to the mind of man."

Still, this departure does not greatly help the Christian.

It is by no means an intention of the present writer to blaspheme Christianity. But it is necessary to swoop in on some logical, rational truths in the context of our discussions that may not be hugely pleasant to the conventional Christian dogmatist. Firstly, the notion that Adam and Eve behaved in a disgustingly sinful manner behind the back of a spotlessly benevolent God in the Garden of Eden is not as black and white as many would suggest. Adam and Eve were formed, initially, as two innocent and unspotted beings, but, in their pre-creation stage, can we honestly claim, in these same conventional terms, that there existed a similarly innocent and unspotted God?

Hadn't God foreseen the descent into Sin that awaited his pending human creations? Didn't he foresee the earthly punishments that they had to look forward to? Despite an omniscient foreknowledge of the failure of his Edenic enterprise, and the realisation that Adam and Eve would suffer terribly for that failure, didn't God conjure Adam and Eve nonetheless, and, more than that, situate them in the particular circumstances that pointed the way to their Fall? It was God's own decision to set the inevitable tragedy in motion, and to watch as man dispatched himself to earth in order to atone for his immorality.

To be brutally honest, if an entity other than God had been the omniscient being to set the ball rolling in the GodàAdam&EveàFall sequence, humanity would have passed the buck and placed the greater blame on this other entity's head long ago! Moreover, logic forces the conclusion that in instructing man to go forth and be Good, an equally true reading of God's sermon is the instruction to go forth and be Evil, for without Evil the co-dependent concept of Good becomes a nothingness and we tumble, therefore, into an animalistic pit of moral Indifference akin to the one we have spoken of above.

This great quandary of Good versus Evil swings us back now to our rope and to Aestheticism, which can offer us a helping hand in all this.

We know by now that followers of Aestheticism posited the contemplation of Beauty as being their chief goal in Art, and that they made the pursuit of pleasure a main fondness in everyday life. Drawing on our woven rope, we find that this coheres nicely with our Neo-Platonian delight in the contemplation of ideal Beauty, and with our Epicurean dedication to pleasure. But before Aestheticism can help us with our moral dilemma of Good versus Evil, we must first ask, and solve as best we can, a very important literary problem. The problem is this:

Aestheticism was associated with what is described as 'Decadence' in Art, and the two words ('Aestheticism', 'Decadence') are often used synonymously in reference to the same artistic works, or even to the same Art movement. This synonymity has often puzzled scholars and Art enthusiasts alike. Our challenge is to make sense of the fact that Aestheticism presented an artistic attitude that was more completely absorbed in Beauty than any other before or after it, whilst Decadence, as the term suggests, connotes a pallid attitude of decay and rot, which essentially undermines everything that a Cult of Beauty could conceivably worship.

How can two such contrary artistic qualities possibly be in any way synonymous?

This is an important conundrum in the context of the moral concerns outlined in this essay, for reasons that will become clear. Therefore it is by no means a waste of time for us to take a brief aside here in order to deal with it directly.

The word Decadence, in moral terms, has intensely negative connotations, and refers to the condition of falling away, or of breaking down, or of decay, but as with many Art History words, the definition can only be looked up in a dictionary in part; the rest of one's grip on the meaning must be built up by experiencing and understanding the artistic work of the Decadent movement first-hand. This predicament has caused many people, particularly academics, to misunderstand the significance of Decadence in Aestheticism.

In the first essay of RKR Thornton's *The Decadent Dilemma* (London, Edward Arnold, 1983), for instance, we find a classic example of such error. Thornton, working from a sort of 'dictionary' understanding of the word, sees 'Decadence' as representing the exact opposite of 'progress'. This is fundamentally incorrect in the Art History context in which Thornton employs the term. Moreover, in viewing Decadence, in the context of Art, as symbolising the other side of the coin of 'progress', we witness the errors that can arise in the misapplication of binary logic. Thornton writes about an 'England of Aestheticism' era - Aestheticism, it will be remembered, flourished in the Victorian period - that has fallen into both a state of, and, importantly, an attitude of, decline; and he sees the arty expressions of decay in Decadence as symptomatic of this. He essentially presents the reader with a bi-polar binary of progress/Decadence.

The blunt truth is that the Victorians did not have an attitude of decline. Indeed, the Victorians probably represent that which is taken as conventional modern 'progress' at its epitome. Bertrand Russell in his History of Western Philosophy writes of the Greek Golden Age that "the achievements of Athens in the time of Pericles are perhaps the most astonishing thing in all history", and elsewhere in the same book writes that "[the] age of Pericles is analogous, in Athenian history, to the Victorian age in the history of England", likening the great Golden Age of Athens to the British Victorian era, which Thornton would mistakenly have us believe to be some sort of example of the very opposite of 'astonishing' progress.

The Victorian outlook did perceive a world of progress: it was embodied in the boundless development of the Industrial Revolution; in Imperialist British expansion; in the concept of progress offered by Darwinism, where the continually self-bettering evolutionary process and progress become two inextricably linked phenomena; and in the prevailing Christian piousness of the era, which offered people the certainty of progressing towards fulfilment in a blessed afterlife.

The main puzzle we face in getting to grips with Aestheticism has little to do with a false sort of Victorian social decline. Our major task is to address the paradoxical synonymity between Aestheticism and Decadence, as outlined in the question some paragraphs previously. Here it is again:

Our challenge is to make sense of the fact that Aestheticism presented an artistic attitude that was more completely absorbed in Beauty than any other before or after it, whilst Decadence, as the term suggests, connotes a pallid attitude of decay and rot, which essentially undermines everything that a Cult of Beauty could possibly worship.

What does our special philosophical rope reveal to us in all this? A particular series of philosophers have been drawn upon that express the central role of pleasure to human existence, as tempered by a moral propensity for Good. In Aestheticism we encounter an Art movement that generalises the vast pleasures of the world, both intellectual and bodily, under the heading of Beauty. Life presents man with a series of Beauties, which, if we take an Epicurian initiative, we may revel and delight in. It is here that we touch on the secret of Decadence, for the decay that Decadence embodies is not some superficial decay of Victorian society as academics have often contended, it is a decay of morality: it is a decay of love into hate, of God into Satan, of light into dark, life into death, attractiveness into repulsion, in short, of all things Good into all things Evil.

Yes! Beauty, like all the elements of a binary, is incomplete without its opposite. And how should we best generalise that great opposite? How do we describe it? 'Ugliness', perhaps? Or 'decay'? No- for the sake of aesthetic symmetry, let us generalise Aestheticism's great dark Other, that seering embodiment of all things devoid of Beauty, of all things reviled, as horrid, contemptible 'Disgust'.

Thus, the co-dependent binary of Beauty/Disgust bespeaks of that pleasurable element in life, be it mental or sensual, as well as of its dark, co-dependent and relational cousin, decay. Hence, no wonder that the seemingly contrary worlds of the Beauty of Aestheticism and the disgust of Decadence become confusingly merged in literary history. That is the reason why Decadence and Aestheticism are inextricably linked, and it is also why the movement produced work of such wondrous artistic excellence.

Only a deep genius truly humbled by the paradox of Aestheticism's Beauty/Disgust could sum up the great tragic glory of our Beautiful, Decadent existence...
as Baudelaire does here in a fabulous passage from *The Desire to Paint:*

> Unhappy perhaps is the man, but happy the artist, who is torn with this desire.
> I burn to paint a certain woman who has appeared to me so rarely, and so swiftly fled away, like some beautiful, regrettable thing the traveller must leave behind him in the night. It is already long since I saw her.
> She is beautiful, and more than beautiful she is over-powering. The colour black preponderates in her; all that she inspires is nocturnal and profound. Her eyes are two caverns where mystery vaguely stirs and gleams; her glance illuminates like a ray of light; it is an explosion in the darkness.
> I would compare her to a black sun if one could conceive of a dark star overthrowing light and happiness...
> ...There are women who inspire one with the desire to woo them and win them; but she makes one wish to die slowly beneath her steady gaze.

Now we can return to the dilemma of the Good/Evil binary armed with the profundity of Aestheticism. As with Zoroaster earlier, not to mention Epicurus and Plotinus, it says a lot for the old wisdoms that we also bring the first significant piece of Art-criticism ever written into the discussion at this point, namely, Aristotle's Poetics.

CATHARSIS

In *Poetics* Aristotle explores the subject of emotion, and he situates his theories in the context of drama. Aristotle concludes that if we go to the theatre to see a tragedy we are experiencing events that in normal life should be deeply, appallingly upsetting to us; but because we watch them at their remove from the real world on the stage, our emotions are aroused in a way whereby negative feelings, like pity or terror, are helpfully purged. Simply put, the Art of drama allows the audience to exercise negative emotion in a safe environment.

Let's take Romeo and Juliet as an example of how this works. The tragic deaths of Romeo and Juliet hardly make for a 'happy ending' to Shakespeare's great work, yet we come out of the theatre satisfied that we have had a very enjoyable evening's entertainment. What in real life would be a series of negative experiences, such as the deaths of certain characters, or the bigotry towards one another exhibited continually by the Montagues and the Capulets, or certain social and gender prejudices that various characters display- all of these things, which in real life would upset us, somehow become part of the overall pleasure of the theatrical experience; and hence, the exercising of our negative emotions becomes a part of the pleasure itself.

Aristotle described this purifying or relieving of the emotions by Art as catharsis. Let's just dwell for a moment on what a staggering property of Art we have brought into focus here. Human beings contain rich vats of emotion, and these vats sometimes bubble up uncontrollably, and at times these vats can overboil and, in their worst forms, bring ruin to a person's day, or week, or even one's very life. Entire wars have been started by these bubbling vats. How often do we find it splashed across the front of the papers that someone has been beaten to death by a gang overcome by the emotion of anger? How often has the emotion of misplaced pride caused some foolish band of politicians to bring international relations to a dangerous fanatical apex?

Surging emotion is a deep, inextricable part of human nature. Indeed, it is one of the qualities that actually make us human. To crush our emotional propensities would not only be impossible, but would lead to the crushing of our very own human natures. How remarkable is it then, and how valuable is it to us, that the Arts can provide a sphere where we may exercise the depths of our emotions in ways that are safe, non-damaging, and even, it cannot be denied, in a way that brings us into contact with that most splendid of all Epicurean delights, pleasure!

Art, then, provides a sphere distinct from the reality of our everyday world where the negative areas of the human condition can be exercised in a positive way, thus giving the human being an outlet for his or her negative aspects whilst simultaneously making the dangers they present harmless and safe. It is of no surprise to us, therefore, that we live in an age where an emergent area called Art Therapy is breaking through, in which Art becomes a kind of medicine and healing tool for people with a whole range of psychological and other ailments. What modernity calls Art Therapy, the Ancient Greeks called catharsis.

Art, it seems, has a great value in attending to the conflict between negative and positive emotion, or what Spinoza called virtuous emotion and dangerous passion, but what, then, does it have to say for that most vital of ethical areas, the moral dilemma of Good versus Evil?

Man as a species is a moral race, and one that inherently believes it is best to be Good. This inherent belief that we 'should' or 'must' - or, as Kant said, 'ought to' - try and be virtuous is held by Christian, Atheist, and Agnostic alike. The Christian analogy drawn upon earlier has been used as a kind of tool to express how man, a species comprised of morally Good Individuals, has been located within a world that conspires against him. God made us Good, but knowingly set events in motion that were to cast us into sinfulness; and the very world we inhabit, hinged around innate Evil as well as innate Goodness, just as Zoroaster expressed it all those centuries ago, actively conspires against our moral efforts. And our problems are not only external. A person's internal world acts against him too, for though the vast majority of Individuals intend to be Good, the quality of Evil inherently impinges on the inward intentions of the virtuous. In short, and drawing again upon the ideas locked into the fibres of our rope, we may conclude that the human race is at bottom a Beautiful species living in a Beautiful world, but one that must nonetheless battle against the natural circumstances in which it finds itself.

This is our great ethical challenge.

ART AS FUNCTIONAL

In a world that necessarily calls upon the existence of both Good and Evil, the ideology of Art as catharsis allows us to suggest a solution to nothing less than man's greatest ethical problems.

We have discussed how negative emotions, associated with the undesirable side of the great moral binary of Good versus Evil, can be actively stimulated in the realm of Art in a safe, therapeutic way. This leads on to a particular solution to ethical problems. If we consciously feed motifs, themes, and emotions themselves that are specifically associated with Evil into the sphere of Art, we should find that the undesirable qualities existing in the artistic forms will continue to be made considerably less harmful via catharsis. If, on top of this, we consciously reduce negativity as much as we can in our everyday world, we should find that the necessary qualities associated with the Evil side of our moral binary will be flourishing safely in Art whilst simultaneously being reduced in everyday life. Decadence is therefore relocated from the real world into the Art world.

Essentially, the great effort here centres on the conscious channelling of negativity and badness out of the everyday world and into the world of Art. Within the world of Art this moral darkness and decay can be left to jostle and struggle against artistic Beauty. The artistic realm makes the experience of negativity safe, reducing the immediacy and the danger of badness via catharsis without causing goodness to suffer unduly also. If 'badness' can be consciously transposed to the aesthetically transcendent sphere of Art, where it is made safe, we can allow a purer form of 'goodness' to persist in the real everyday world in which we live, thereby, as the old cliché goes, making our world a better place.

This happy state of affairs allows Evil to be present in Art as a conception, and even as an actual quality of experience, and this is a very positive thing, for Evil must exist in human experience in order for Good to exist. With the negative aspects of human morality being filtered through the safe-making Imaginative artifice of artist-and-audience, the real world around us is freed up to become the conscious domain of Good. Indeed, pushing the hypothesis to its idealistic peak, we might well be able to bring human morality in the everyday world as close to a state of pure goodness as is rationally possible.

In the real world, our everyday lives, we are unwise and self-destructive if we pit ourselves in the pursuit of challenging God or demon; but in Art, Faust can challenge the very fabric of God himself, and the reader / theatre audience can collude in the sinful story cathartically. In life, then, goodness and morality are free to reign supreme. The necessary Evil, the negative impulses in our natures, may be compressed into Art, where we can exercise the full range of human emotion and experience in a positive way.

For sure, the new conditions brought around by such gradual repositioning of Evil into the cathartic sphere of Art will certainly insist upon a degree of restraint on the part of the artist's audience; excessively 'bad' Art (as in 'Evil') will no doubt have an ability to bring terror to the very fore of the human consciousness, and in doing so it will allow the terrible experiences and actions depicted in Art to become a conscious psychological possibility in the human mind. This could potentially influence susceptible people in dangerous directions.

Thus the human mind must continue simultaneously to cultivate its capability of restraint, and in certain cases it may be that a degree of censorship ought to be roughly proportional to this capability (which will naturally differ somewhat across, for example, certain age groups). In this respect goodness/badness are in a sense empirical - we learn limits of Good and Evil, and must develop restraint in order to cope with them.

(A great deal more could be said on restraint, and particularly on the matter of censorship, the latter being an area where the meddling of politicians, the pious moral majority, and so forth, have continually undermined great Art across the ages; but we must press on here with the main avenue opened by our thinking and save such asides for another day).

By chance, it is Aristotle again who can help us frame the implications of these ideas for both our everyday lives and for Art itself. This time we turn to his concept of the golden mean. According to this rule, a virtue is the midway point between two extremes, each of which is a vice. 'Modesty', for example, is a desirable half-way point between the two undesirable extremes of 'Shamelessness' and 'Shyness'. Aristotle believes that if we attain a balanced personality, we will also attain happiness in life. In many ways, this is a splendid idea for getting through a healthy, happy life, and is, to a long way, to be recommended.

Art, however, is a different matter. As our friend Jeremy Bentham puts it, "wars and storms are best to read of, but peace and calm are better to endure." As a cathartic sphere, and as the plane where the Imagination of the great artist is given free reign, in Art the golden mean most certainly goes out the window. In fact, we find an ideal approach to Art being that which can approach the extremes of a binary, and therefore Art takes a stance in direct opposition to the golden mean. We are talking about Art in the tradition of Rousseau here. A great novel might take us to the very heights of Beauty, then dash us on the rocks of disgust, and we are all the richer for the experience.

One masterful sweeping epic poem might explore all the themes that are great in human nature, and another might explore all the things that are the most base. Clearly, to create Art that probes complex intellectual ground, and that also explores its geographical cousin, the great mountainous lands of the emotional high and the emotional low- to create Art, we are saying, that touches the very depths of our souls, we require the work of imaginative genius. It is impossible for an Art that aims to make room for man at his most Good and his most Evil to be anything but extreme in one way or another.

To summarise, we have built up a conception of Art as functional here. Art provides a cathartic plane where the artist's ingenious Imagination may conjure up both the myriad world of Beauty, and its necessary co-dependent twin, the misty world of disgust. In doing this, Art enriches our experience of living whilst also purging and purifying the human psyche so that we can get on with living virtuous, genuine lives, lives that attempt to avoid dangerous, destabilising extremes, but that gently and continually press towards the Good side of moral action.

SOME CONCLUSIONS

We have just travelled on a rich voyage, and the following destinations have formed the skeletal locations of our journey.

Creative Imagination
          ...located within...
the Individual
          ...part of a world hinged around...
Binary Opposition
...the presence of Evil leading to...
Catharsis
          ...the neutralisation of negative morality via its relocation into Art leading to...
Art as Functional

Beginning with the smallest of elements involved with our being alive - the Creative Imagination of a single human being - the above series of intellectual progressions is followed through till one arrives at the idea of the Arts as playing a vital, functional role in human Ethics. In order for goodness to exist in our world our existence must be bound up with an inescapable and simultaneous sense of badness, and Art can provide a cathartic plane where negative ideas and emotions can be purged in a comparatively non-harmful way. In consciously shifting qualities associated with ethical badness into Art, and in trying to replace the resulting vacuum by encouraging goodness in our everyday lives, Good and Evil can continue to co-exist, as indeed they must; but the quality of Art has gained in richness from the transposition and the everyday world has gained in virtue from the withdrawal of negativity. As new highs of Beauty and new depths of disgust are being plumbed in the world of Art, new goodnesses can be plumbed in the real world around us.

ENDNOTE
Some Thoughts for Students of Literary and Cultural Theory

A literary student puzzling over the reinstatement of values and ideas associated with Aestheticism that, let there be no mistake, this booklet entirely encourages, or an Arts addict contemplating the way in which the ethical perspectives laid down here intend to make Aestheticism current again, might mentally associate the liberal results of these intentions with the sort of pre-theory phase of literary criticism characterised by IA Richards' *Practical Criticism* and the like. In one sense, this association is a fair one to make, but in another sense it is false also. Perhaps the main departure (though by no means the only one) from that old-school kind of theory is the insistence here that Art must be elevated to a cathartic plane entirely above conventional social morality. We can call it a cathartic plane in an Aristotelian sense, and an amoral, Decadent plane in a Wildean sense. Either way, the point is clear.

Aside from not being able to accommodate the advances in theory that came after them, the interpretations offered by Richards, and others like him, especially FR Leavis and the rest of the old-school crew of critics that closely followed Aestheticism in the progression of literary history, are what one might describe as too 'realist'. For instance, when critics analyse a text like Henry James' *The Turn of the Screw*, much tends to be made of the several narrative shifts in the text that distance the reader from the actual events in the story as they occur. This is a fair point as far as analysis goes, but the modern Aestheticist would stress that all Art exists at a great shift and displacement from the reader, regardless of the additional self-reflexive shifts that can be charted in pieces like James' story.

Indeed, Art is as far from real life as man's most fantastical inner imaginings are from the mundane, outward world that surrounds him. Therefore, a realistic Leavisite reading that attempts to essentially 'judge' Art within a sphere of conventional moral principles is thoroughly flawed, and the tinge of moral prescriptivism that haunts the admittedly crudite and thoroughly interesting writing of Leavis goes horribly against the grain of Aestheticism's faith in cathartic function. On the cathartic plane we may celebrate Good and Evil, Beauty and Disgust, in a sinless, cathartic way.

Hence this style of Aestheticism's reinstatement of the idea that all excellent Art is in some way Decadent.

We also gain a new appreciation in all this for a writer like Sir Philip Sydney, the first important name in English literature to stress that a chief purpose of Art should be to give a reader pleasure. To the pious Christians surrounding him in the abstentious Sixteenth Century, and to those taken by certain popular books, such as Plato's *Timeaus*, which had described pleasure as the greatest incitement to Evil, Sydney said "hey! Relax a bit! It's ok to have fun with the Arts while we're alive here" (to paraphrase his points in the *Apology for Poetry*).

We will find ourselves when all these things are said and done with a good deal to think about in terms of contemporary Art theory and the ways in which we look at the world. In 1981 the French writer Jean Baudrillard published a book called *Simulations* where he argued that the cultural images we're constantly bombarded with, such as the ones on TV, have disturbed the gap between what's real and unreal to the point that reality has collapsed and a 'hyperreality' now exists in its place.

Amongst all this Baudrillard contended that the 'real' Gulf War never actually took place, and that instead there was merely a sort of televised non-real depiction of a virtual reality. Needless to say, to the soldiers out getting blown to bits in the Gulf, the war must have seemed very 'real' indeed. Baudrillard is misguided in pushing his theories too far, which, as this booklet insists, has been an unfortunate vogue in philosophy since time immemorial.

This is merely one of many instances where a sort of theoretical 'compromise' is called for, a softening of the rigid, totalising application of new theory. We also observe here that such a stance might easily be mapped onto people who seem extremely removed from the qualities we associate with the Good part of our Good/Evil ethical binary. The similar denial of the Holocaust on the part of certain Neo-Nazis will spring to mind.

An example like Baudrillard on the Gulf War illustrates theory's current distance from the real world. In its increasingly abstract state, critical thinking has distanced itself from life so that it exists only in the mind of a few philosophers and some scholarly papers. Indeed, it could be argued that philosophy is more pervasively abstract at present than it has ever been before in lieu of the advent of deconstruction, which has had the effect of making abstract philosophy even more abstract through its methods of breaking down meaning in texts. It will be interesting to see if theoreticians will be able to turn this all around and make vital contact with life as a lived process again. It will be quite a challenge...

NEW AESTHETICISM

When I was in the late stages of my BA degree at Queen's University Belfast (2003), some student friends and I, with the support of particular lecturers and established writers, founded an Arts Collective called The Knights of the Round Table. We had been strongly inspired by the Victorian 'aesthetic movement' and I encouraged my friends to refer to our attitudes to the Arts as New Aestheticism. My philosophies on Art have developed in conjunction with my work as President of this Arts Collective, and so I have stuck to our expression, New Aestheticism, and introduced it formally for the first time in this booklet.

Unbeknownst to us, however, a small field within academic research calling itself New Aestheticism was coming into being at virtually the same time that our Collective was developing. Inspired by Jonathan Loesberg's *Aestheticism and Deconstruction: Pater, Derrida, and de Man* from Princeton University in 1991, it's a very recent development that has found its fullest voice to date in The New Aestheticism edited by John J. Joughin and Simon Malpas in England 2003.

For the reasons above, and for the literary and philosophical reasons occurring within this book generally, I have decided to keep the term New Aestheticism. The *New Aestheticism* of Joughin and Malpas is relatively little-known at present, is purely academic, and deals with the whole thing on a specialised, strictly theoretical level; this approach is entirely different and separate to the New Aestheticism laid out in this book.

TLM
(Belfast, November 2004

Thomas L. Muinzer

AFTERTHOUGHTS ON THE ARTS

If we are to be in keeping with these ideas, the Arts should have a shape and substance and should be far, far removed from the airy waffliness, the insubstantial intellectual conceits, the overdone realism, the unfocused flab of much of what characterises contemporary 'modern' Art. Contrary to popular belief, the artist owes an audience little or nothing; it is the audience that must owe the artist a debt. The artist therefore has a responsibility to the profession of 'artist' itself, and must act responsibly, work responsibly, create Art responsibly. In short, he or she must be an authentic artist.

It is time to stop asking what life can show Art, and start asking what Art can show life.

In all this, as we feed our highs of Beauty and lows of Decadence into Art, we must do our utmost to ensure that life is feeding this to the sphere of Art, and that Art - the Decadent sort at least, if not the Beautiful - is spilling as little of its negativity as possible back into the real world in which we live. (A great deal more may be said on this matter, but it is a discussion for another time) This will be a great challenge.

These ideas introduce a New Aestheticism.

TLMuinzer,
Belfast,
January 2004

On Ethics